# THINGS I'VE THOUGHT TO TELL YOU SINCE I SAW YOU LAST

By the same author:

*The Unlikely Orchard*

*Suburban Anatomy*

# THINGS I'VE THOUGHT TO TELL YOU SINCE I SAW YOU LAST

## PENELOPE LAYLAND

RECENT WORK PRESS

Things I've Thought to Tell You Since I Saw you Last
Recent Work Press
Canberra, Australia

Copyright © Penelope Layland, 2018

ISBN: 9780648257929 (paperback)

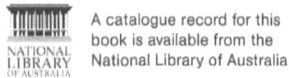 A catalogue record for this book is available from the National Library of Australia

All rights reserved. This book is copyright. Except for private study, research, criticism or reviews as permitted under the Copyright Act, no part of this book may be reproduced, stored in a retrieval system, or transmitted in any form by any means without prior written permission. Enquiries should be addressed to the publisher.

Cover design: Recent Work Press
Set by Recent Work Press

recentworkpress.com

*For Melissa and Catherine Wellham*

# Contents

| | |
|---|---|
| Future anterior | 1 |
| In Miss Havisham's garden | 2 |
| Calendar | 3 |
| A modern offer | 4 |
| Rising of the Lights (London, 1665) | 5 |
| Aubade | 6 |
| Irregular | 7 |
| One Tree Hill | 8 |
| By request | 9 |
| Breath – Relief | 10 |
| Pearl | 11 |
| Cowries | 12 |
| Cold zeal | 13 |
| Terror management theory | 14 |
| Avalanche | 15 |
| Birthday video | 16 |
| Caul | 17 |
| Life after television | 18 |
| There is no ease in water | 19 |
| Painting the wind | 20 |
| Pre-ceremonial | 21 |
| Atheist in the cathedral | 22 |
| Revenant | 23 |
| This loss | 24 |
| Surface and shadow | 25 |
| *Veteris vestigia flammae* | 26 |
| Last night | 27 |
| Fit for this | 28 |
| Roland Barthes' mother in the Winter Garden, and other photographs | 29 |
| Phoenix | 31 |
| About my cat | 32 |
| Pluto | 33 |

| | |
|---|---|
| Year three | 34 |
| *Lacrimae rerum* | *35* |
| Curracurrang | 36 |
| Contracture | 37 |
| Fixity | 38 |
| Currawongs at minus 6 | 39 |
| Sky burial | 40 |
| Marigold | 41 |
| One year and nine months | 42 |
| String | 43 |
| Overboard | 44 |
| Light | 45 |
| The angry men's ward | 46 |
| Death bed | 47 |
| Friedhof der Namenlosen | 48 |
| Tintinnabulation | 49 |
| Conjugal headstones | 50 |
| A long time | 51 |
| Wish you were here | 52 |
| J. M. Barrie's boys  (in the Everest death zone) | 53 |
| The garden before what happened in it | 55 |
| Something lost | 56 |
| The Ly-ee-Moon Cemetery, Green Cape, NSW | 57 |
| Brooch | 58 |
| Ash, dust | 59 |
| Write you | 60 |
| I went today | 61 |
| Case | 62 |
| *Timor mortis conturbat me* | 63 |
| Die like a dog | 64 |
| The inverted gaze | 65 |
| Things I've thought to tell you since I saw you last | 66 |
| | |
| Afterword | 68 |

## Future anterior

The trees wear their mortality
bare to the breezes,
skeletal behind their fig-leaf of leaves.
Their bones show brittle
and decay nestles in pits of their
stretched limbs.
Even the Huon, reptilian with age,
shows in standing
a stricken shape.
In the quiet breath of midday
it is majesty and ruin under one crown.
In high wind it wrings its hands
in a fussy froth, saying
*I will have died.*

## In Miss Havisham's garden

The swimming pool of collected summers
is opaque lime under charcoal clouds.
Loose skeins of butterflies unweave in air.

We have been dismantling your traces,
putting away tools that fitted your palm
like a puzzle completing,
smoothing webs from mowing machines
while sasanqua relinquish
their sogged and blousy buds.

In the soil are the marks of you still:
spade slice; impress of hand about the bulb.
Last year while roses whetted new thorns
to be tempered by the frost
your rooms reeked of winter jonquils.

Now the jonquils are cocooned.
Drowned mice are dredged from the pool.
Sasanqua drop and shatter on dropping.
Twice daily I sweep the terrace of their flesh.

## Calendar

The early months of your death
are booked up well in advance:

golf club lunches that won't be eaten,
a birthday to be missed,

standing dates to be stood up:
salon—dentist—specialist.

There are library books to be unread
and a fridge festooned with lists

of errands, theatre visits,
ideas for perfect Christmas gifts.

The pool man comes tomorrow,
the gas bill on the 3rd.

The Sunday paper skips the lawn
till stopped by the fishpond rocks—

we must remember to cancel it
(and the milk, and the post-office box).

Now we're answering Christmas cards
conveying your unwelcome news again.

Next year's calendar is propped by your phone,
sealed in cellophane.

### A modern offer

Dispensing
for argument's sake
with the whole
harp-and-cloud version
and putting aside
squeamish concerns
about corporeality
and the passage of centuries

and confining ourselves
to a more
contemporary rendering,
involving an ill-articulated
celestial soup
of remnant consciousness—
a kind of
resistless
merging of essences,

why then
is there not
panic on the streets
at the prospect
of eternal life?

## Rising of the Lights
## (London, 1665)

Childbed. Teeth.
Stopping of the stomach.
French pox.
Frightened.

Smallpox. Flox. Grief.
Found dead in the street.
Bleeding.
Griping in the guts.

Drowned
(one at Stepney,
one near the Tower,
one Westminster).

Imposthume.
Quinsie. Rickets.
Stranguary.

Head-mould-shot.
Surfeit.
Stone.

Kings evil.
Timpany. Worms.
Rising of the Lights.

## Aubade

It's mostly in this falling season,
walking out early,
that I've seen the horizon's bright seam
in those slow seconds to dawning,
the thread of incandescence
that ruptures into morning.
And then, so quick, the spatial shift:
hardening light about my feet.
Daybreaks past and future stretch
each side of one indrawn breath.

## Irregular

The verb 'to mourn' has too many manners,
is uttered by ladies fingering old photos
or sighing over letters from the front.

There's nothing mannerly in this:
my breath punched out at the traffic lights;
surging from sleep with a throatful of horror.

I need a verb with steep sides
and a brutal rap of consonants.

A cliff of a verb
to knock against, with fists.

## One Tree Hill

We do not watch the news nowadays
and have stopped buying papers.
But still our hilly, gusty conversation turns
on what we say we want to avoid:
madness of kings, the insufficiency of outrage,
the fact that all this is all there is.

Toward the top, speech gets harder
and we find what we came for,
things we can re-imagine later,
things that may survive this poem:

flanks of hill clotted with wattle
like eruptions through the skin of the lemon sun,
and the brahminy kite, poised forever on a bulge of air.

## By request

No Calla lilies whitely fleshly
hours from pooling, darkening at the edges
or masking violets massed and corrupting sweetly.
Nothing with eyes that stare brightly
or button-like or deep jet-lashed or dewy.
Nothing nodding, nothing proud,
no thorns so no roses.
No garden sprays careless with infinite care
or lavender like clothes packed away.
No primrose, for there'll be no spring.
Bring no white chrysanthemums.
Perhaps poppies, kind oblivion.

## Breath – Relief

The air tonight seems made
half of sighs
half of held breath:

one part expectation
one part grief.

If it were colder
my exhalation might wreathe
your turned-away temple;

adhere, a faint frieze
telling of love beyond telling

and beyond retrieval.
I expect you any minute—
outside of belief.

# Pearl

After you left the bed I could still feel the length
of your thigh along mine,
the passive, resting pressure, a dry warmth.
So long as I remained motionless
you were both *here*,
between the closed lips of sheets,
and *there*, in the shower,
the shifting patterns of splash that I sometimes,
half-awake, mistake for rain.
The sheets cooled but your leg remained:
actual, tactile, in my skin memory,
an old scar that does not mean pain,
just a tightness, an awareness.
This is not a love poem, or not only a love poem,
or a love poem but not only for you.
I have to tell you
this happens more and more:
your absent clench in the small of my back
while I hear you filling the kettle,
your lips on my shoulder
as you sip the wine,
even my own parts on my own parts:
ankle fitted on ankle,
uncrossed but still feeling crossed,
the small, double-crossing disorientation
of moving an arm which isn't where it felt I felt it was.
Watching my hands in the mirror, cack-handed,
or your hands on my neck
in a mirror also, clasping, unclasping, reclasping the pearls.

## Cowries

A man meets us going the other way, from Angourie,
says he's already mined the good spots,
the swirl and lick at the foot of boulders and driftwood.
I imagine him combing the incoming slick
like a parent smoothing hair with fine fingers.

My mother too has the action,
there she is, while he speaks,
sweeping with her thin cramping hands
to untumble a damp stillness beneath.
Her time is eked for all purposes. One is sifting for shells.

As the man wanders on, she holds to the light
a cracked clamp of chinaware,
an almond unzipped.
It is slippery on her thumb,
tumbles back to shingle.
Her hand dips again without hesitation.

## Cold zeal

Eyesight fails, and the compass
of the immediate world shrinks.
Once, glances were cast out
far and with a practiced flick
and the bounty was hauled back in beauty—
in ice etchings on a paling fence
or the oily swirl
of a river's revealed currents,
brief looks of interest from strangers,
the complexities of mist.

## Terror management theory

this singularity

we carry
like an egg or a rock

hating the weight
fearful of a knock

but it's hard to
live so mindfully
and get much done

so mostly it's like
breath or pulse:

forgotten
till it's not

## Avalanche

I fear death by drowning.
Also by fire,
slow cancer,
or swift brain bleed.
Mid-summer
or else in May.
I fear dying alone
or watched.
I fear death on a Tuesday
or other day.
Car crash,
crane drop,
the plunging plane.

## Birthday video

I don't recognise anyone.
Not you, beardless and smiling,
with sadness in your eyes
and babies like koala young
attached to your back,
nor the one that must be me—
I would have been there
on a day like that.

There's no fond nostalgia in this—
*don't we look young!*
*haven't we gone to fat!*
Just fretfulness
at friends lost gone
or forgotten gone, good-riddance gone
or dead gone,
and my dead father's voice,
which I'd forgotten I loved,
just singing a foolish song.

## Caul

First to pass this way today
I break through wetly
night-spun webs
and make for my face
a silken caul.

Midwives tell
that those born capped
will never die of drowning.
But still I gag,
nostrils grabbing,
eyelashes frantic
as insects
fallen into suspension.

Even when
the sunlight comes,
alarming each trip-wire,
still they rip and clutch,
laying on crossed,
clammy hands,
saying
*there are more ways*
*to die dry*
*than there are to drown.*

## Life after television

We look at pictures of log fires
to feel warm
while the wind swallows all sounds
smaller than its own
and flicks petals from the geranium.
*What do we now think
about this or that?*
I'd make a cake by hand
the ache of wooden spoon
pulling elastic batter.
We might have eaten it
at the table, swept crumbs
into our palms.
But we've awakened a need
that cannot be tidied or quieted or exhausted
and that cannot be fed at all.

## There is no ease in water

Even glass-cast, blood-warm,
it takes just a spoonful to perfuse the lung.
Face-down, I watch grey things scuttle
in a swirl of gusted sand
and listen to my breath, intubated, rattle.

All my growing years,
routine as bath or bed or prayer
was the night sound of your muffled wet cough
and my mother's percussive fists,
as she pressed your perished bellows
into another year or two of breath.

Beyond the coral, surf is thudding.
The sun refracts in molten folds.
A small fish holds itself steady,
with fractional flicks of gauzy fins,
and looks me in the mask.
His gills gulp the golden water.

## Painting the wind

Each few seconds
the wind bulges.

Glass cannot keep it
walls cannot

out of my sleep
my sighing

the sound and compression
the pressure of it.

You wrote, once,
about painting the wind.

I cannot write it now
without you oozing in.

## Pre-ceremonial

All the way
across town
following the hearse
we are on display
behind the windows
of the family wagon
washed for the occasion.

Only three streets
from there to there
and we travel them so slow
with headlights on
though it's summer
with cicadas.

Three streets of strangers
standing sentinel
hands clutching papers
snatched from the lawn
or the dog's lead, tensed
against misbehaviour.
Joggers awkward with ear-buds
and songs suspended
and men with idling,
burbling mowers.

We travel them so slow
with the headlights on
and the streets are filled
with stilled figures
stumbling into something
not quite part of them.

## Atheist in the cathedral

That spring,
as every September,
the sky was deceitful

blue, buds knocked up
by imperative rhythms,
knocked down by ice.

The worm was
at me, mouthing.
Fretful morning showers

had me tasting rust.

## Revenant

How now, are you
back then
after some months
forgetting?
The dead hand
on my morning,
the prick to my dream.
I had thought this
worked out, and
you seen right through.

## This loss

is not to share,
must be furtive
and unsaid.

There is no headstone
for estrangement,
no dead.

No postings in the press
no public rites.
But at the thought

of you
my lung
is tight laced

with black crepe,
bombazine,
the light-sucking stuff.

## Surface and shadow

Leaner,
far longer at first light,
a Giacometti striding,
you pace me,
not grating or creaking or tripping
but rippling over the rocky hill.

At the summit we stop:
I to breathe; you because
you're shackled to me.

The sun goes higher
quicker than you think.
You shorten, plumpen,
more like me now.

Slump here awhile, then,
grass for hair
a broken parrot wing
scarlet at your brain pan,
small pebbles
where a heart.

### *Veteris vestigia flammae*

Sometimes there beckons
from cold morning ashes
a parched, bleached afterimage
of what was consumed—

a gnawed bone,
bent as if for kissing,
the shape-ghost of a log,
long sinews miraculously intact.

But no warmth—
at the touch of a finger
all atomises to creaking dust.
The fragile softness disgusts.

## Last night

    she sat near
        but not touching
            as slow blood mottled
                in your fingertips and
            in the fringes
        of your ears.
She said you
        used to take her
            to the picture show
                years ago
            and in the back row
       in the white flicker
of forgotten scenes
        on remembered screens
            you would pare and slice
                an apple
            with your pocket knife
        handing her
cool slivers
        solemn as
            gift-wrapped
                chocolate.

## Fit for this

The hill is steeper this morning.
Even the dog seems to feel it.
Late acacia is freighted
with heavy, graceful heads.

You've the look of new knowledge,
wear the shoulders of someone older.
Grey is green, the air is smell,
Hardenbergia is where it hid.

I'd trade this fizzing spring
for one proper, aching wind
to alert the breath in your nostrils,
remind you what winter really is.

# Roland Barthes' mother in the Winter Garden, and other photographs

At Chennevières-sur-Marne, aged five. Acute elbows, a calyx of white collaring her throat, one finger hooked in the other fist. Buckled shoes a burr of just-stopped scuffing. Hair a spiky, sepia twist. Mildly round-eyed as though someone has just made an offer, in return for attention. This is what Barthes finds among his mother's things. The details, I confect.

*Napoleon's brother, Jerome, in 1852. Well-fed, sleeked hair and a top hat tilted on a white thumb. Exhausted about the mouth, the look of one who has just exhaled. No need for confection — this image exists. Google it. Barthes' one thought: 'I look, in this image, into eyes that looked into the eyes of the Emperor'. He is astonished, mentions it at evening parties, with intensity. People remember that they were just on their way to get a drink.*

The Winter Garden has tropic palms, glass refractions that bewitch shutter timings and a smell of quick and wet decay. There's a sweating ornamental bridge in the background; in the foreground, near Barthes' mother's five-year-old cheek, a smudge that may be something dark on the wing, or an artefact of the darkroom. What will be lost when this is all gone into the bin or the fire when Barthes dies? Not the smudge. I imagined it.

*Lewis Payne, failed political assassin, 1865. Lurched against a plate-metal wall, he could be a propped post-mortem portrait for the papers, but this happens to be pre. He is angelic, in looks. Cleft chin. His hands are a pianist's. His shirt strikes the eye like a swipe of velvet. Barthes: 'I observe with horror an anterior future of which death is the stake'. Both 'this will be' and 'this has been'.*

There's an older brother, aged seven, arm extended along the rail of the ornamental bridge. He's turned away, swiftly, so his chin has the sheered look of a landed uppercut. She, Barthes' mother, aged five, has not noticed, attention fixed *mostly* on whoever's behind the lens, talking, and *a little* on her right stocking, which is relaxing into white ruches below her knee. Barthes shows us every photo but this one: the Winter Garden, the gasping palms, the bright glass canopy. The point is, she is going to die. It inheres in every photo, this catastrophe.

# Phoenix

Here is the instinctiveness of the old salmon, heaving upstream to spawn, flesh already turning mush, burrowing magnetically through the ripping, flaying water.

Here is the self-knowledge of the ageing, drowsy queen, signing her own black warrant, squatting out virgin rivals even as the murmurous workers cluster for the regicide.

He assembles fragrant, volatile twigs of cinnamon. His scaly neck snakes this way and that, his old eyes roll with knowledge of what is to come. From his beak drip flames, low and cool, that suddenly take.

## About my cat

For reasons unexplained my tea is gouts of silent rising steam. Summer evening, with a beanie on my head and a cold patch on my lap. Absurd, but I worry about the steady rain, how it will trickle down that foot or two like a drip down a neck, to where we put her, just now, after so long being dry and here and warm.

## Pluto

We knew it would end like this. At the rough and ragged end I even dreamed it, looked for it, forward to it. It took one hour to wish it all undone. This is not you being on Pluto, not you with a flat phone battery, not you ignoring me.

## Year three

Descending to the coast, she detects through a whistle of car window the same outbreathed eucalypt that eddied hotly across a fibro room at Pretty Beach, the afternoon of your first crisis, blood frightening on a white pillow. Flowering gum, with a hot, drab hanging of leaves. Disinfectant. In the glove box, a disc you burned on a boozy night. Your voice cracks through cheap speakers. The dogs lift theirs from the backseat, in counterpoint.

## *Lacrimae rerum*

The genitive engenders ambiguity.

Tears *of* things. A foetal moon, shielding its black, empty belly. A juddering forest, blossom sodden. A cascading howl of wolves, unheard for centuries, now shattering their silence upon your small head.

Tears *for* things: I take lament into my own hands, the sugar and fat of sentiment. Tears for you, *thing*. And for the vanished wolves, for Europe's lost forests, for the moon robbed of mystery.

Mostly for you, deemed too small for formal reception, certification. Though your fingernails were softly, perfectly formed, your eyes a real blue behind your sealed lids.

# Curracurrang

After several hours of walking, a place of hard red rock, where a trickle of tea-dark water composes itself in shallow handfuls before tilting toward the cliff. Earlier, at Bundeena, 'missing-person' posters for a teenage son had frayed from telegraph poles and utility boxes. While I recover my breath, a stiff wind sheers up the rock-face to catch the fresh water as it tips over, lifts it back in particles, makes it mist, held aloft by physics, or wishing.

## Contracture

Her bass-clef hand is narrowing at the palm. Every few months another semitone is unreachable and she's hopping like ragtime to cover the loss. The surgeon gives her a leaflet, describes the zigzag incisions, says it means she has Viking blood, though she's never felt less red-headed. Back home she breathes in the blistered varnish, felted hammers with their faint, plosive dust, the acidulous brass of the pedals, the glottal silence.

Early on, they had spent a year in York, for his work. Tight with distaste and disappointment, she had paced the museum. Her memories are of bones—whistles, cracked from the legs of songbirds, and a wishbone bridge for a Viking lyre.

# Fixity

Algorithms insist that this image on my screen has not altered by one pixel, that the burn of your cheek is as fresh, the bleed of sweat on your mare's flank is as dark, her eye as rolling. I'm almost out of the frame, one sandaled ankle in a stirrup. The stirrup is the stirrup it was, exactly. Your hair, I see now, is more halo than afro, but afro or halo enough for a white girl with thin, red arms, hauling in a sweating mare with rolling eyes unaltered, though the horse must have been for the knackery these 40 years, or tractored into a pit on the bottom paddock.

## Currawongs at minus 6

Saline pushes like a small, cool tide up the arm to the elbow, where it is distinguishable no longer. The drug follows the same path, but stinging and slower. Outside, minus 6, but the furnace of infection is cosy. Currawongs exclaim, but only about the weather.

# Sky burial

She will be bird-scattered. In gentleness, body-breakers will feel for where the joints are resistless. Where there's no wood for wasting or soil for concealment, death becomes an act of generosity, fealty to quick seasons, sudden-wilting meadows. Rock, rock. Pelting, rainless clouds. This land needs all the death it can get. Vultures spiral into unstoppable decline. Parents of dead infants sometimes quail, instead set sail tiny boats with light burdens into the runs of milky ice-melt, where fishes feed.

# Marigold

The ghat is kept for the highest caste, but they lave her in the river as though she needs cleansing. Nearby, a child bobs and sinks in the lumber and fatty swirls, then emerges, sleek, unclean as a river thing, to squat and watch.

White as a faintness, limbs restlessly anyhow, mouth keeps opening but eyebrows quite concentrated. White without light. Old, or looking old, now.

The wood is laid about in intricate structures, a perfect lie. The mound of garlands is teased apart and strung. The oldest son sets the flame. For a long while, the fire and the marigolds are the same.

## One year and nine months

One year and nine months and he has not stopped moving—places you were together, and ones intended. In his pocket, zip-lock bags of you, small rubble, gritty dust, uncompromising, as in life. You have been snatched by the wind at Machu Picchu, furtively dumped at Gracelands, have accreted the fields of Civil War dead and fallen noiseless and twisting from the cliffs at Royal. Today, you anoint Karl Marx's grave at Highgate (also, the bust of Bruce Reynolds, mastermind of the Great Train Robbery, but not the cool, shadowed plinth of George Eliot). The historian in you would be tickled, I think. Resting on a bench crocheted with lichen, by the plain stone of Sidney Nolan, he says, *you should really talk about this stuff. We didn't.* Next week he takes you to Auschwitz.

# String

Tidying, I find under the sink a jar labeled in bluing ink: *'Pieces of string too short for normal use'*. Driving home, the feel of her narrow shoulders still in my palms, I think of her slow, spatulate fingers moving with the muscle memory of trussing a chicken's bald ankles, garroting the throat of a pudding calico, bracing the brittling tomato vines with their unripe fruit. Jobs for string sufficient to the task of Cat's Cradle, a scaffolding for brown-paper parcels, an emergency plait for wind-whipped hair, a lace for a loose-tongued shoe. What to do, then, with those shorter lengths? The pointless, the purposeless, the leftover? In the length of my drive I think of just two: the making of a bouquet of her spare keys, for my bottom drawer; and a bow for my forefinger, to keep attention upon what might otherwise be casually forgotten.

## Overboard

To be always within hearing
of the gull's desolation,
within reach of this sea
of greasy basalt
where the midnight sun
spreads thinly portside
and squid-ink impenetrable
to starboard.
On the stern deck,
from which he leaves
in a swift and controlled vault,
the ropes are coiled,
like serpents wrestled
and won
earlier from the deep.

## Light

How then,
when she was so light
that enfolding her
was cupping a brittle bird,

when her clothes swaddled her
and her food was pecked
and shifted about the plate,
when even her eyes grew a lighter blue,

how then is her coffin so heavy
at her dying
that I struggle
to hold my end of it?

# The angry men's ward

Women die more neatly, as a rule—at the first stroke.
Men are higher maintenance:
the young dive into shallows or drive into posts.
The older encounter smaller obstacles—
tiny clots jamming brains, efflorescing bleeds.
They rage at the untidiness,
at the sturdy arms that roll and strap them
into contraptions of pretended mobility.

'I'm a master mariner,' they spit.
'I'm a professor of English Literature.
I've dropped bombs, drawn a crowd,
built a sideboard, changed oil,
toileted without a guiding hand,
done without this cheery pity.

I've had women look at me not *at* me'.

## Death bed

takes on new meaning here,
where every bed is purposely designed
and fit for the purpose.

Your mattress is made of pneumatic cells
that sigh and bloat
to vary the pressure on skin thinner
than skin-thin.

You don't so much sink as float,
remote, shape-shifting,
an idea of restlessness.

You'll leave no impression
of your own, but be exhaled
with bed-mates unknown
in thin streams of having been,
the mattress quiet in between.

## Friedhof der Namenlosen

The Danube is not blue and does not dance
but surges green with snow-melt
toward Simmering where it flattens, slows
and a meander lets go of the coarser silt,
the storm-wrenched things:
old barrel staves and bloated sheep,
Vienna's murdered and its suicides.

Plant them where they've come ashore,
in the black alluvial dirt,
a cobbled communion of crucifixes
each hung with a gilded Christ.
Equality in him and anonymity.

*Speak your name, for you cannot be recognised.*
'No name, no name, even before the river took me,
rolled me in the greenness of cold.
My name was left on the last bridge,
in the stones sewn into my pockets,
the ligature about my throat.'

## Tintinnabulation

They say the time
        How late the day
The time in the day
        The wind in the hour
Of wind when it
        Pushes down and in.

Clamorous, they
        Speak in tongues
Of frailty, fealty
        Tongues of coldest
Oldest bronze.

There's no not-hearing.
        No deal can be struck.
The child is fled
        The windflower plucked
The father dead.
        Just as they say

Unspeakably.

## Conjugal headstones

Doubly wretched,
a shared grave unshared:
stone sculpted in expectation,
a ditch double-depth dug.
A splayed page engraved,
but one side forever undated—
a century's lichen can't obscure:
this bed's half-empty, un-mated.
It speaks unwonted happy endings,
re-marriage, removal, release
for she who held a ripening hand,
looked into a cooling eye,
swore she'd go to the lip of dark
and join him by and by.

## A long time

Eternity is a long time for anything:
to be in love without outwearing welcome,
to be dreamless without hope of dreaming,
to remain interested.
To do without the escape of exhaustion,
or the small deceit of pretended sleep.

## Wish you were here

Houses hold fast through habitation:
walls will stand while there's breath within,
but chaos has an instinct for an opening.

Vandals, moulds, are agents of entropy,
silence is a start—enough to crack the windows,
and alert the termite.

Week one: dust flocculates,
a stripped mattress jangles with sudden springs.
The violin lets itself go by half-tones.

Your things are becoming just things.

## J. M. Barrie's boys
## (in the Everest death zone)

This air is thin as gruel.
One after another they taste it—
the faint, oatmeal slipperiness,
the cold that shocks the pink of the lung.

This one, his boots acid yellow as a builder's vest
palms prayered around an absent coffee,
head could be dozing, wind fingering
the fur of his hood, like breath.

Another, there, has toppled
into eternal youth, hip-splayed
the width of a double bed
in eddies of duckdown,

head proffered in profoundest sleep,
snow packing his parted lips.

> *Tupac, Norbu, Mallory, Irvine*
> *Wilson, Wang, Breitenbach.*
> *By avalanche, haemorrhage, exhaustion,*
> *fall.*

The inessential is lost first:
digestion, love, logic,
chunks of Milton, periodic tables,
a best dog's name.

Next lost are the extremities:
will, anger, a wife's face.
Life's companions fall away
like beads from a snapped string.

> *Lobsang and Tasker, Lhakpa, Pasang,*
> *by perishing wind and swollen brain,*
> *crevasse and ice-fall.*
> *Eyes open to the passing years,*
> *cheeks cryonically palled.*

Some are now become way-markers:
'bear right at red jacket,
right again at the ice cave'
into which one crept
flag stitched to his breast,

to realise he was solid to the calves,
to catch and lose his breath.
No telling from the faces
how shrunken necessity feels.

## The garden before what happened in it

The roses blew redder.
There were more birds then.
No seasons, but abundance
year-round.

The fish faced no predator,
permitted the sun
to flash its swift flanks
like a wound.

Perfection was sedative
but curiosity wormed in.
The resting tyrant woke
at the sound.

## Something lost

Safe outside and in
what we have lost is half of heaven
the dark half, the half light, the dark against which
the light of creation still streams,
the black pelt of 2am with galaxies thrown across it.
All auroras, low lustres, enfolding ink washed away,
no match for the street light, headlight, lamppost
the hand-holding city, the amber for idling
the low glow by the cot
so the baby will not wake
to the terrible knowledge that the night is dark.

We are un-enfolded. We are laid out and stark staring.
We are as the crippled bat, blundering into black rock
the deafened dog that fails to heed the silent whistle.

# The Ly-ee-Moon Cemetery, Green Cape, NSW

The clearing is hemmed solid with twisting banksia
and a coming tempest's thickened air.

They hauled the bodies here
brined and laundered
to be always within hearing
of the thing that killed them:
the concussion of water and rock.

Green Cape Light sweeps a clockwork eye
but quick, quick, quick.
It is not a searchlight,
cannot fix upon a point,
upon one figure torn away
one trapped by the shoulders in smothering foam,
another snatched from rescue's arms
and given up to rock.

Some are named here, others not.
For each, one simple, whitewashed rock:
the cook's friend;
a woman, unaccompanied;
the man with the German accent.
Their psalm is the seasonal cicada,
the susurration of small birds,
the booming bell of water-beaten rock.

Over the century, sand has shifted.
Finger bones have reached for finger bones,
pelvises tilted, craniums touched.

## Brooch

Would I want a brooch
of your human hair
if that was all I had of you?

Send me the brooch
with the plait tight-woven of silver-grey
smoothed with your sweat.

Would I want a diamond
pressed of your carbon
if a ring was all that remained of us?

The diamond would shine clean white
inside the greasy plait tight-woven.
Send it to me.

Would I want your leg-bone,
the long one of your lean and silky-haired thigh
to poke my embers into heat?

Poke, poke, shed light
on all the glittering facets
inside the greasy plait.

Would I keep you from the ground
or from the flames
to keep from losing you forever?

Undig the darkening earth.
Extinguish the heat.
Let us lie, cool, on the surface of things.

## Ash, dust

Again, beloved, sum a human worth
in these two dates: Death and Birth.
Graven in stone or memorial wall
each man's measure
measured in things
common to all.

*Un*mention all that is tenuous—
the sudden and unbidden glimpse:
opera of erupting calyx,
the wrestle in a gaping gill,
jasmine through a night-propped sill,
blue pulse in a turning wrist.

The moments most devoutly sought,
and most reluctantly unheld,
the things most meant, the things most fated,
here lie spent, undated.

## Write you

To remember your laugh
I walk out into a shrilling dawn
where currawongs soul-whistle
as they swoon from trees
and the dog breathes complexities
from a blade of grass.

To recall your eyes I find
any cracked old leather chair and sit
till my heart slows
to the thick knock of seconds
at the case of your mantel clock.

To hear your breath
I need a winter wind
finding ways around
summer's muscled obstacles,
startling skin to rise
and moaning of the great effort of life.

## I went today

again down to where
willows trawl the dark water
and moorhens startle every time
as if for the first time
from the cold, clattering rushes.
Went down seeking
not the willows' deep-reaching,
but forgetfulness, like birds.

## Case

In the bag of effects
are your cold dentures, clicked away
in a jaw-shaped case.

Click.

They smell
of breathing out,
of the soft opening of an armpit
at the last
to reach for the cool,

of the *pah*     *pah*
of puffed, sleeping breath.

## *Timor mortis conturbat me*

Faith is most faint
in this hour before dawn.
A sigh might extinguish it.

On the wards it's the death-watch,
the deep ebb.
The cooling perfume of breath
settles like a gauze.

Let me die just so,
in faithlessness and fear,
fully alive
to what's being lost,
not dreamless as a baby
or taken unawares.

## Die like a dog

Dog does not die,
is merely there, then not—
depthless eye shallowed,
become loveless,
tongue loosed.

Death's dominion
depends on attention.
He gave it none—

neither this one
nor the small death
attendant on each
moment

walk
ball
bush
bone

## The inverted gaze

Is it a trick of composition
or of light
that you catch and hold my eye
from your hallway frame?
I recall that sitting:
a last corralling
of our generations.
In seven days you would be dead
and look not at all
like yourself.
Tonight, your eyes catch
at those of the living,
anxious to tell something,
or curious,
or just communing,
or none of these things,
simply lost in thought
or simply lost.
You gaze still,
looking longest,
long after I've looked away.

## Things I've thought to tell you since I saw you last

How the first sun of summer is
a red hand on my shoulder.

How cheese can be:
shattered, corrupted,
or bulging from its skin.

That I thought I saw you looking
from my dog's liquid eye.

How, after all, it was only my dog,
bone-lust and loyalty
in dangerous, delicate balance.

## Afterword

The poems in this collection are a sidelong, oblique bid to explore the enduring power of elegiac poetry in a secular age. Dispensing with God, they do not, I trust, fully dispense with faith.

The poems attempt to engage with aspects of the elegist's preoccupations: the power of naming; the impermanence of memorialisation; the conviction that nature itself partakes in our grief (and the equally compelling conviction that it does nothing of the sort).

These and other elegiac conventions have been developed, tested, queried and challenged by poets from the earliest times, but have never been fully abandoned. Their invocation links the elegist writing in the 21st century to others who have responded to their own losses and griefs throughout human history. This is the language of ritual, the act of mourning itself.

Perhaps this is why elegiac poetry is still able to console and satisfy, even when the traditional consolations - assurances of heaven, eternal life and reunion - are no longer available to the secular poet. The ritual has been enacted, the words have been written. The memorial will not last. The words will finally fade or fall from use, but the work of mourning will have been done.

# Acknowledgements

Most of these poems were written as part of a practice-based PhD I undertook at the University of Canberra. My research was generously supported by the Australian Government's Research Training Program, for which I am extremely grateful.

A number of the poems, while broadly 'on-topic', arose from an international prose poetry project also operating out of the University of Canberra, of which I have been a very small part.

Thank you to Professor Paul Hetherington, my primary supervisor, and to editor Shane Strange, for taking a risk with a collection so unrelenting in its preoccupation.

And thanks and eternal friendship to all past and current members of the Molonglo Writers. We have shared wine, cheese and our work in progress for many years, and I for one have met with nothing but kindness, encouragement and, best of all, criticism.

A number of the poems in this collection have been previously published.

*Westerly*—Roland Barthes' mother in the Winter Garden and other photographs

*The Canberra Times*—Timor Mortis Conturbat Me

*Tract* (Recent Work Press)—Contracture, Fixity

*Spun* (2012 University of Canberra) —In Miss Havisham's Garden, Friedhof der Namenlosen

*Pulse* (2016 Recent Work Press)—Sky burial

2018 Editions
*The Uncommon Feast* **Eileen Chong**
*Inlandia* **KA Nelson**
*Peripheral Vision* **Martin Dolan**
*The Love of the Sun* **Matt Hetherington**
*Ley Lines and the Rustling of Cedar* **Niloofar Fanaiyan**
*Things I've Thought to Tell You Since I Saw You Last* **Penelope Layland**
*Moving Targets* **Jen Webb**
*The Many Uses of Mint* **Ravi Shankar**
*Abstractions* **Various**

2017 Editions
*A Song, the World to Come* **Miranda Lello**
*Cities: Ten Poets, Ten Cities* **Various**
*The Bulmer Murder* **Paul Munden**
*Dew and Broken Glass* **Penny Drysdale**
*Members Only* **Melinda Smith** and **Caren Florance**
*the future, un-imagine* **Angela Gardner** and **Caren Florance**
*Proof* **Maggie Shapley**
*Black Tulips* **Moya Pacey**
*Soap* **Charlotte Guest**
*Isolator* **Monica Carroll**
*Ikaros* **Paul Hetherington**
*Work & Play* **Owen Bullock**

all titles available from
www.recentworkpress.com

www.ingramcontent.com/pod-product-compliance
Lightning Source LLC
Chambersburg PA
CBHW032049290426
44110CB00012B/1012